# Guided Reading Study

Inside Earth

PRENTICE HALL Science Explorer

PEARSON

Prentice Hall

Needham, Massachusetts
Upper Saddle River, New Jersey

ISBN 0-13-190173-7          1 2 3 4 5 6 7 8 9 10    07 06 05 04 03

# Inside Earth

**Guided Reading Handbook . . . . . . . 5**

## Plate Tectonics

Earth's Interior . . . . . . . . . . . . . . . . . . . . . . . . . .9
Convection and the Mantle . . . . . . . . . . . . . . .13
Drifting Continents. . . . . . . . . . . . . . . . . . . . . .16
Sea-Floor Spreading . . . . . . . . . . . . . . . . . . . . .18
The Theory of Plate Tectonics . . . . . . . . . . . . .21

## Earthquakes

Forces in the Earth's Crust. . . . . . . . . . . . . . . .26
Earthquakes and Seismic Waves. . . . . . . . . . .30
Monitoring Earthquakes . . . . . . . . . . . . . . . . .33
Earthquake Safety . . . . . . . . . . . . . . . . . . . . . . .36

## Volcanoes

Volcanoes and Plate Tectonics. . . . . . . . . . . . .41
Properties of Magma . . . . . . . . . . . . . . . . . . . .44
Volcanic Eruptions . . . . . . . . . . . . . . . . . . . . . .47
Volcanic Landforms . . . . . . . . . . . . . . . . . . . . .52

## Minerals

Properties of Minerals. . . . . . . . . . . . . . . . . . . 58
How Minerals Form . . . . . . . . . . . . . . . . . . . . 62
Using Mineral Resources . . . . . . . . . . . . . . . . 65

## Rocks

Classifying Rocks. . . . . . . . . . . . . . . . . . . . . . . 71
Igneous Rocks . . . . . . . . . . . . . . . . . . . . . . . . . 75
Sedimentary Rocks . . . . . . . . . . . . . . . . . . . . . 79
Rocks From Reefs. . . . . . . . . . . . . . . . . . . . . . . 84
Metamorphic Rocks. . . . . . . . . . . . . . . . . . . . . 87
The Rock Cycle. . . . . . . . . . . . . . . . . . . . . . . . . 90

**Science Explorer** • *Reading Skills Handbook*

# 🐟 Target Reading Skills

## Identifying Main Ideas

To get the point of what you are reading, you need to identify the main idea. The main idea helps you understand what the reading passage is about. Sometimes that's pretty easy to do. For example, suppose you are reading just one paragraph. Very often you will find the main idea in the first sentence, the topic sentence. All of the other sentences in the paragraph provide supporting details or support the ideas in the topic sentence.

But don't be fooled. Sometimes the first sentence is not the topic sentence. Sometimes you may have to look a little deeper. In those cases, it might help to read the paragraph and see whether you can summarize what you have read. If you can, then you have the main idea.

Of course, a textbook has many paragraphs, each one with its own main idea. However, just as a paragraph has a main idea and supporting details, so does the text under each heading in your textbook. Sometimes the main idea is the heading itself. But sometimes it's not that easy to find. You may have to infer a main idea by combining information from several paragraphs.

To practice this skill, you can use a graphic organizer that looks like this one:

## Outlining

A good way to see how supporting details relate to main ideas is to make an outline. It's easy to make an outline as you read. Using this skill can actually make you a more careful reader.

Your outline can be made up of sentences, simple phrases, or single words. What matters is how the parts of the outline relate to one another. To outline while you read, use a plan like this one:

I.  Section Title
   A.  Main Heading
      1.  Subheading
         a.  detail
         b.  detail
         c.  detail

If you need to, you can step your outline out to yet another level by putting supporting information under each detail. When you outline in this way, you are deciding just how important a piece of information is. Is it important enough to list under the subheading? Or does one detail actually support another detail?

| Main Idea | | |
| --- | --- | --- |
| Detail | Detail | Detail |

**Science Explorer** • *Reading Skills Handbook*

## Comparing and Contrasting

You can use comparing and contrasting to better understand the relationship between two or more concepts in a reading passage. Look for clue words as you read. When concepts or topics are similar, you will probably see words such as *also, just as, like, likewise,* or *in the same way.* When concepts or topics are different, you will see *but, however, although, whereas, on the other hand,* or *unlike.*

To use this skill, it sometimes helps to make a Venn diagram. In this type of graphic organizer, the similarities are in the middle, where the two circles overlap.

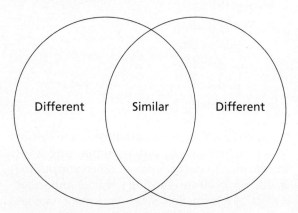

## Relating Cause and Effect

This skill looks at a different sort of relationship that you will see while reading. Cause-and-effect relationships are a very basic part of science. A cause is what makes something happen. An effect is what happens. In science, many actions cause other actions to occur.

Sometimes you have to look hard to see a cause-and-effect relationship in what you are reading. However, just as with comparing and contrasting, you will find clue words to help you identify causes and effects. Look for *because, so, since, therefore, results, cause,* or *lead to.*

But watch for more. Sometimes a cause-and-effect occurs in a chain, with an effect becoming a cause of later effects. You can see these relationships more easily if you use a graphic organizer like this one:

| Cause |
|-------|
|       |
|       |

→
→

| Effect |
|--------|
|        |
|        |

## Asking Questions

The material in your textbook is organized under headings and subheadings. You can prepare to read the material under those headings by turning each heading into a question. For example, you might change the heading "Protecting Yourself During an Earthquake," to "How can you protect yourself during an earthquake?" Asking questions in this way will prepare you to look for answers in the reading material. You can use a graphic organizer like this one to ask questions:

| Question | Answer |
|----------|--------|
|          |        |
|          |        |
|          |        |

**Science Explorer** • *Reading Skills Handbook*

# Sequencing

Sometimes when you are reading, you will find clue words that tell you the sequence or the order in which things happen. You see words such as *first, next, then,* or *finally.* When a process is being described, you might even see numbered steps somewhere in your reading. But you can't always count on having these clues provided for you. Using the sequencing reading skill will help you understand and visualize the steps in a process. You can also use it to list events in the order of their occurrence.

You can use a graphic organizer to show the sequence of events or steps. The one most commonly used is a flowchart like this one:

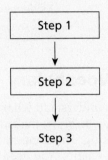

Sometimes, though, a cycle diagram works better:

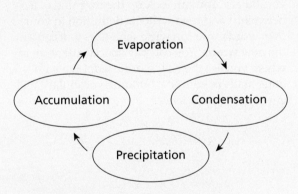

# Using Prior Knowledge

Use this reading skill to relate what you are reading to something that you already know about. It's easier to learn when you can link new ideas to something that is already familiar to you. After all, if you don't have the background, you probably won't fully understand what you

are reading. For example, if you don't know that fish are actually breathing oxygen that is dissolved in water, you won't fully understand how or why gills work. You might need to know about how gases dissolve in water, how lungs compare with gills, how oxygen is used by an animal's body, and many other useful bits of prior knowledge.

Using prior knowledge can help you make logical assumptions or draw conclusions about what you are reading. But be careful. Sometimes your prior knowledge might be wrong. You can figure that out, too. As you read, you can confirm or correct your prior knowledge.

You can use a graphic organizer to link your prior knowledge to what you are learning as you read.

| What You Know |
|---|
| 1. |
| |
| |

| What You Learned |
|---|
| 1. |
| |
| |

**Science Explorer** ▪ *Reading Skills Handbook*

## Previewing Visuals

Most people agree that looking at pictures can make learning about a new topic much easier. When you flip through a section of reading and look at the visuals, reading labels and captions, you get a pretty good idea of what the reading is going to be about. For example, if you preview the visuals in a chapter about volcanoes, you will see more than just photographs of erupting volcanoes. You will see maps, diagrams, and photographs of rocks. These might tell you that the reading will discuss where volcanoes are found, how they form, and what sort of rock is created when volcanoes erupt. This preview might make you more prepared to understand and enjoy what you are about to read.

One way to use this strategy is to look through the material you are going to read. Choose a few photographs, diagrams, or other visuals and write questions about what you see. Then answer the questions as you read.

## Identifying Supporting Evidence

When you are reading about science, you will often read about a hypothesis. A hypothesis is a possible explanation for scientific observations made by scientists or an answer to a scientific question. A hypothesis is tested over and over again. The tests may produce evidence that supports the hypothesis. When enough supporting evidence is collected, a hypothesis may become a theory.

Identifying supporting evidence in your reading can help you understand a hypothesis or theory. Evidence is made up of facts. Facts are information that can be confirmed by testing or observation.

When you are identifying supporting evidence, a graphic organizer like this one can be helpful:

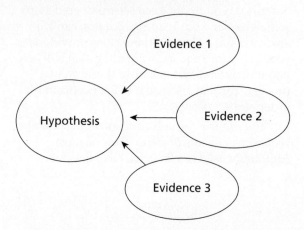

## Building Vocabulary

Before you can understand what someone is saying, you have to know the language that person is speaking. The same rule applies to understanding science. You need to know what the words mean.

There are many ways to build your vocabulary. You can look up the meaning of a new word and then write its definition in your own words. You can write sentences that contain the new words. You can pay special attention to where you see the new word used. Like with other skills in your life, building vocabulary will get easier with practice.

# Earth's Interior

*This section explains how scientists learn about Earth's interior. The section also describes the layers that make up Earth and explains why Earth acts like a giant magnet.*

## Use Target Reading Skills

*Before you read the passage for each heading, fill in the top box with what you know. After you have read the passage, fill in the bottom box with what you have learned.*

| What You Know |
|---|
| I. Earth's crust is made of rock. |
| 2. |
| 3. |
| 4. |
| 5. |

| What You Learned |
|---|
| I. |
| 2. |
| 3. |
| 4. |
| 5. |

## Exploring Inside Earth

**1.** What prevents geologists from directly exploring Earth's interior?

_____

_____

**2.** Geologists use direct evidence from _____ to learn about Earth's interior.

**3.** Geologists learn about Earth's interior using indirect evidence from

_____.

Name _____ Date _____ Class_____

**Plate Tectonics** · *Guided Reading and Study*

## Earth's Interior (continued)

4. Is the following sentence true or false? Earth looks the same today as it did millions of years ago. _____

5. Seismic waves reveal the structure of Earth through their _____ and _____.

6. Circle the letter of each sentence that is true about Earth.

   a. Indirect evidence of Earth's interior comes from studying rock samples.

   b. Geologists cannot observe Earth's interior directly.

   c. It is over 6,000 kilometers from the surface to the center of Earth.

   d. Geologists learn about Earth's interior by drilling holes.

7. _____ waves are produced by earthquakes.

## A Journey to the Center of Earth

8. How does the temperature change as you go from the surface toward the center of Earth? _____

   _____

   _____

9. How does pressure change as you go from the surface toward the center of Earth? _____

10. The three main layers that make up Earth are the _____, _____, and _____.

## The Crust

11. The _____ is a layer of rock that forms Earth's outer skin.

12. Is the following sentence true or false? The crust is thinnest under high mountains. _____

13. The dark-colored rock that makes up most of the oceanic crust is _____.

14. The light-colored rock that makes up most of the continental crust is _____.

**Plate Tectonics** ▪ *Guided Reading and Study*

## The Mantle

Match the name of each layer of the mantle with its description.

**Layer**

___ **15.** lower mantle

___ **16.** lithosphere

___ **17.** asthenosphere

**Description**

**a.** Rigid layer that includes the upper part of the mantle and the crust

**b.** Solid material beneath the asthenosphere

**c.** Soft layer just below the lithosphere

**18.** Is the following sentence true or false? The asthenosphere is not considered solid because it can bend like plastic. _____

**19.** Is the following sentence true or false? The mantle is nearly 3,000 kilometers thick. _____

## The Core

**20.** Circle the letter of each sentence that is true about Earth's outer core.

    **a.** It is under low pressure.

    **b.** It is made of solid metal.

    **c.** It contains iron and nickel.

    **d.** It behaves like a solid.

**21.** Circle the letter of each sentence that is true about Earth's inner core.

    **a.** It consists of molten metal.

    **b.** It behaves like a thick liquid.

    **c.** It is not very dense.

    **d.** It is under extreme pressure.

## Earth's Interior *(continued)*

**22.** In the drawing, label the three main layers of Earth.

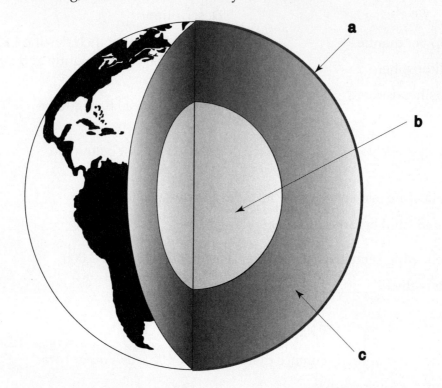

**23.** Describe how a compass needle aligns itself. _____
_____

**24.** What creates Earth's magnetic field? _____
_____

**Plate Tectonics** · *Guided Reading and Study*

# Convection and the Mantle

*This section describes how heat is transferred from Earth's hot core through the mantle.*

## Use Target Reading Skills

*As you read about heat transfer, complete the outline to show the relationships among the headings.*

| Convection and the Mantle |
|---|
| I. _____ |
|    A. _____ |
|    B. Conduction |
|    C. _____ |
| II. Convection Currents |
| III. _____ |
|     _____ |
|     _____ |

## Types of Heat Transfer

1. The movement of energy from a warmer object to a cooler object is called

   _____.

2. List the three types of heat transfer.

   a. _____ b. _____ c. _____

3. What is radiation? _____

   _____

4. What are two forms of radiation? _____

   _____

5. What is conduction? _____

   _____

6. What is an example of conduction? _____

   _____

**Plate Tectonics** · *Guided Reading and Study*

# Convection and the Mantle (continued)

7. What is convection? _____

   _____

8. Heat transfer by convection is caused by differences of _____ and density within a fluid.

9. A measure of how much mass there is in a volume of a substance is

   _____.

10. Circle the letter of the sentence that describes what happens to a fluid when its temperature increases.

    a. Its particles occupy less space.

    b. Its density decreases.

    c. Its particles move more slowly.

    d. Its particles settle together more closely.

## Convection Currents

11. What three factors set convection currents in motion? _____

    _____

12. What happens to convection currents when the liquid or gas is no longer heated? _____

    _____

**Plate Tectonics** ▪ *Guided Reading and Study*

## Convection Currents in Earth

13. Complete the graphic organizer to show the relationships among heat, movement, and density in mantle rock.

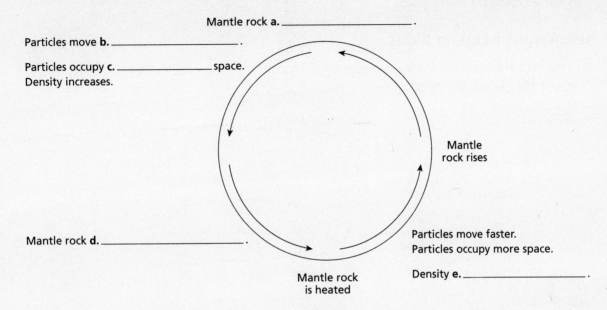

Mantle rock a. _____ .

Particles move b. _____ .

Particles occupy c. _____ space.
Density increases.

Mantle rock rises

Mantle rock d. _____ .

Particles move faster.
Particles occupy more space.

Mantle rock is heated

Density e. _____ .

    f. Why is this relationship shown as a cycle? _____
_____

    g. In the cycle shown, where would mantle rock be the densest? _____
_____

14. Is the following sentence true or false? The heat source for the convection currents in the mantle is the sun. _____

**Plate Tectonics** • *Guided Reading and Study*

# Drifting Continents

*This section describes a theory of how the continents came to be located where they are today. The section also gives evidence for the theory and explains why the theory was not accepted for many years.*

## Use Target Reading Skills

*As you read about the evidence that supports the theory of continental drift, complete the graphic organizer.*

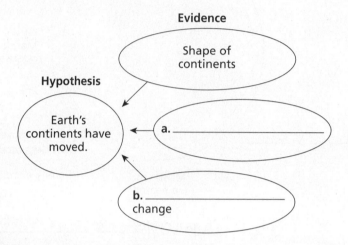

## Continental Drift

1. State Alfred Wegener's hypothesis about how Earth's continents have moved.

   _____

   _____

2. Wegener named his supercontinent _____ .

3. What did Wegener think had happened to this supercontinent?

   _____

   _____

   _____

4. Wegener's idea that the continents slowly moved over Earth's surface

   became known as _____ .

**Plate Tectonics** • *Guided Reading and Study*

5. Circle the letter of each sentence that supports Wegener's hypothesis.

   **a.** Some continents match up like jigsaw puzzle pieces.

   **b.** Different rock structures are found on different continents.

   **c.** Fossils of tropical plants are found near the equator.

   **d.** Continental glaciers once covered South Africa.

6. Give an example of evidence from land features that supported Wegener's idea of continental drift. _____

   _____

   _____

7. Any trace of an ancient organism preserved in rock is called a(n)

   _____.

8. How did Wegener explain similar fossils on different continents?

   _____

   _____

9. Is the following sentence true or false? Wegener believed that Earth's climate had changed. _____

## Wegener's Hypothesis Rejected

10. How did Wegener think that mountains formed? _____

    _____

    _____

11. How do the locations of mountains support Wegener's idea about how mountains form? _____

    _____

    _____

**Plate Tectonics** ▪ *Guided Reading and Study*

# Sea-Floor Spreading

*This section explains sea-floor spreading and describes evidence that it happens. The section also explains subduction and describes how subduction affects Earth's oceans.*

## Use Target Reading Skills

*As you read about sea-floor spreading, fill in the flowchart to show the sequence of events.*

| Magma erupts along mid-ocean ridge |
| :---: |

↓

| Magma **a.** _____ to form new **b.** _____ |
| :--- |

↓

| **c.** _____ spreads away from **d.** _____ |
| :--- |

## Mid-Ocean Ridge

1. Circle the letter of each sentence that is true about mid-ocean ridges.

   **a.** The mid-ocean ridges were mapped using sonar.

   **b.** The mid-ocean ridges are found only below the Pacific Ocean.

   **c.** The mid-ocean ridges are completely under water.

   **d.** The tops of some mid-ocean ridges are split by a steep-sided valley.

2. A device that bounces sound waves off underwater objects is called

   _____.

3. What is sonar used for? _____

   _____

## What Is Sea-Floor Spreading?

4. The process that continually adds new material to the ocean floor is

   called _____.

5. In sea-floor spreading, where does new crust come from? _____

   _____

**Plate Tectonics** · *Guided Reading and Study*

## Evidence for Sea-Floor Spreading

6. List three types of evidence for sea-floor spreading.

   a. _____

   b. _____

   c. _____

7. Circle the letter of each sentence that is true about Earth's magnetism.

   a. At times in the past, a compass needle on Earth would have pointed south.

   b. Rock that makes up the ocean floor lies in a pattern of magnetized stripes.

   c. The pattern of stripes is different on both sides of mid-ocean ridges.

   d. The magnetic memory of rock on the ocean floor changes over time.

8. How did drilling samples show that sea-floor spreading really has taken place?

   _____

   _____

## Subduction at Trenches

9. Deep underwater canyons are called _____ .

10. What is subduction? _____

    _____

## Sea-Floor Spreading *(continued)*

11. Complete the cause, events, and effect graphic organizer to show the relationships among the processes of convection currents, subduction, and sea-floor spreading.

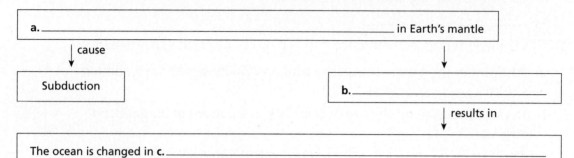

a. _____ in Earth's mantle

cause

Subduction

b. _____

results in

The ocean is changed in c. _____

d. What process in Earth's interior causes subduction and sea-floor spreading? _____

_____

e. What effect do those two events have on Earth's surface? _____

_____

12. Is the following sentence true or false? At deep-ocean trenches, conduction allows oceanic crust to sink back into the mantle.

_____

13. Is the following statement true or false? The Pacific Ocean is shrinking.

_____

14. Why is the Atlantic Ocean expanding? _____

_____

_____

**Plate Tectonics** · *Guided Reading and Study*

# The Theory of Plate Tectonics

*This section explains how the lithosphere is broken into separate sections that move.*

## Use Target Reading Skills

Before reading the section, write simple definitions for the words *diverge*, *converge,* and *transform.* You may use a dictionary. After reading the passages that contain the key terms *divergent boundary, convergent boundary,* and *transform boundary,* explain how your definitions relate to these terms.

_____

_____

_____

_____

_____

Write a definition of each Key Term in your own words below:

plate: _____

_____

scientific theory: _____

_____

plate tectonics: _____

_____

fault: _____

_____

divergent boundary: _____

_____

rift valley: _____

_____

convergent boundary: _____

_____

transform boundary: _____

_____

**Plate Tectonics** · *Guided Reading and Study*

# The Theory of Plate Tectonics (continued)

## Introduction

1. The lithosphere is broken into separate sections called

   _____.

2. Is the following sentence true or false? Plates can carry continents or parts of the ocean floor but not both. _____

## How Plates Move

3. What is a scientific theory? _____

   _____

4. State the theory of plate tectonics. _____

   _____

   _____

5. Is the following sentence true or false? The theory of plate tectonics explains the formation, movement, and subduction of Earth's plates.

   _____

## Plate Boundaries

Match the term with its definition.

**Layer**

_____ 6. plate boundary

_____ 7. fault

_____ 8. rift valley

**Description**

a. Deep valley that forms where two plates pull apart

b. Line where the edges of Earth's plates meet

c. Break in Earth's crust where rocks have slipped past each other

9. Complete the compare/contrast table to show how plates move at the different types of plate boundaries.

| Plate Movement | |
| --- | --- |
| **Type of Plate Boundary** | **How Plates Move** |
| Divergent boundary | a. |
| Convergent boundary | b. |
| Transform boundary | c. |

**Plate Tectonics** ▪ *Guided Reading and Study*

    **d.** How are the movement of plates at divergent boundaries and at transform boundaries similar?

_____

10. Is the following sentence true or false? Crust is neither created nor

    destroyed along a transform boundary. _____

11. Most divergent boundaries occur along _____.

12. When two plates converge, the result is called a(n) _____.

13. When two plates collide, what determines which plate comes out on

    top? _____

_____

14. Circle the letter of each sentence that is true about convergent boundaries.

    **a.** Where two plates carrying oceanic crust meet, subduction does not take place.

    **b.** An oceanic plate sinks beneath a continental plate when the two plates collide.

    **c.** Where two plates meet, the one that is more dense sinks under the other.

    **d.** Mountain ranges form where two plates carrying continental crust collide.

15. Was Pangaea the only supercontinent to have existed? Explain your answer.

_____

_____

16. Is the following sentence true or false? The pieces of the supercontinent Pangaea began to drift apart about 225 million years ago.

_____

**Plate Tectonics** ▪ *Guided Reading and Study*

# Key Terms

*Use key terms from the chapter to complete the crossword puzzle.*

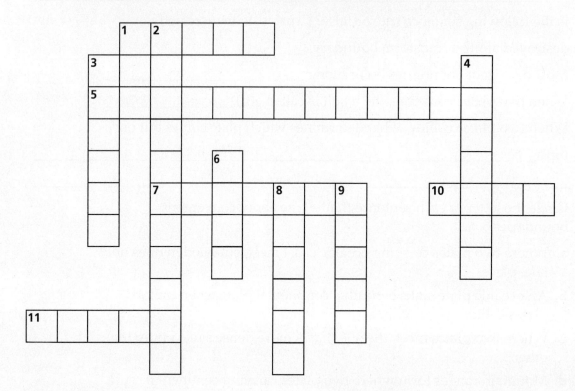

**Clues across**

1. Section of lithosphere that carries crust
5. Part of mantle below lithosphere
7. Kind of wave released during an earthquake
10. The most inner layer of Earth
11. Used to map mid-ocean ridge

**Clues down**

2. Layer that is part crust and part mantle
3. Rock that makes up oceanic crust
4. Study of planet Earth
6. Kind of valley where plates move apart
8. Earth's middle layer
9. Earth's outer layer

# Connecting Concepts

Develop a concept map that uses the key concepts and key terms from this chapter. Keep in mind the big idea of this chapter: Convection currents in Earth's mantle are the driving force that causes the movement of Earth's plates. The concept map shown is one way to organize how the information in this chapter is related. You may use an extra sheet of paper.

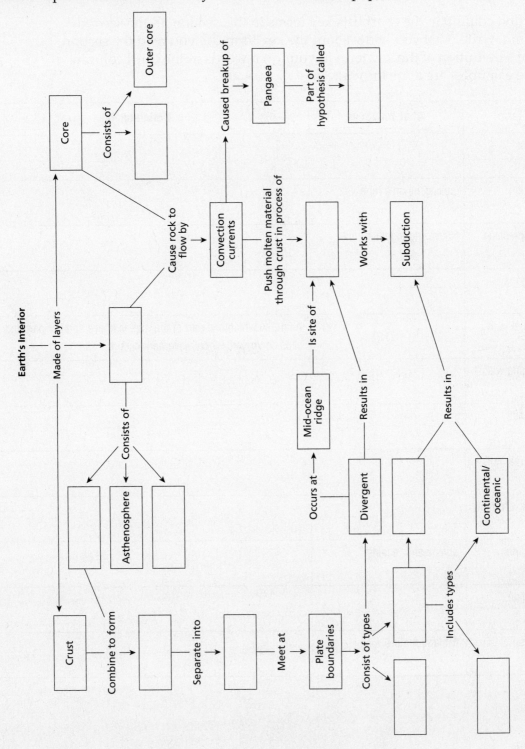

Name _____ Date _____ Class_____

**Earthquakes** • *Guided Reading and Study*

# Forces in Earth's Crust

*This section explains how stresses in Earth's crust cause breaks, or faults, in the crust. The section also explains how faults and folds in Earth's crust form mountains.*

## Use Target Reading Skills

The first column in the chart lists key terms in this section. In the second column, write what you know about the key term. As you read the section, write a definition of the key term in your own words in the third column. Some examples are done for you.

| Key Term | What You Know | Definition |
|---|---|---|
| Stress | | |
| Tension | pulling, as on a rope | |
| Compression | squeezing together | |
| Shearing | | |
| Normal fault | | A fault in which one part of the rock is above another part and slips downward when movement occurs |
| Hanging wall | | |
| Footwall | | |
| Reverse fault | | |
| Strike-slip fault | | |
| Anticline | *anti* means "against" | |
| Syncline | | |
| Plateau | flat land feature | |

**Earthquakes** • *Guided Reading and Study*

1. Circle the letter of the term that refers to force that acts on rock to change its shape or volume.

    **a.** fault    **b.** stress    **c.** pressure    **d.** heat

2. The amount of space a rock takes up is its _____.

## Types of Stress

3. List the three types of stress that occur in Earth's crust.

    **a.** _____ **b.** _____ **c.** _____

4. Complete the cause-events-effect chart to show how the different types of stress change the shape and volume of rock.

| Cause | Event | Effect |
|---|---|---|
| Tension | c. | e. |
| a. | d. | Rock folds or breaks |
| b. | Pushes rock in two different directions | f. |

    **g.** Which two causes can have the same effect? Explain your answer.

    _____

    _____

5. A break in Earth's crust is a(n) _____.

## Kinds of Faults

*Match the kind of fault with its description.*

**Type of Fault**

_____ **6.** strike-slip fault

_____ **7.** normal fault

_____ **8.** reverse fault

**Description**

**a.** The hanging wall slides up and over the footwall.

**b.** There is little up-or-down motion.

**c.** The hanging wall slips downward below the footwall.

**Earthquakes** · *Guided Reading and Study*

# Forces in Earth's Crust *(continued)*

**9.** Is the following sentence true or false? A strike-slip fault that forms the boundary between two plates is called a convergent boundary.

_____

**10.** Circle the letter of each sentence that is true about a hanging wall.

    **a.** It slips downward when movement occurs along a normal fault.

    **b.** It is the half of a fault that lies below in a reverse fault.

    **c.** It is the same as a footwall.

    **d.** It occurs when the fault is at an angle.

**11.** Circle the letter of each sentence that is true about both normal and reverse faults.

    **a.** The faults are at an angle.

    **b.** The faults are caused by tension.

    **c.** The faults are caused by compression.

    **d.** The faults have footwalls.

**12.** Complete the flowchart to show the types of faults and movements caused by stress on rock.

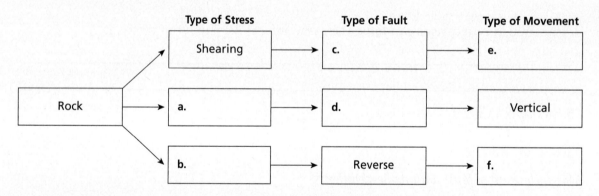

    **g.** Two types of faults can result in mountains. Which are they, and how do you know from examining this flowchart? _____

_____

**Earthquakes** • *Guided Reading and Study*

*Match the landform with the type of fault that produced it.*

| Landform | Type of Fault |
|----------|---------------|
| ____ **13.** San Andreas Fault | **a.** reverse fault |
| ____ **14.** Rio Grande rift valley | **b.** strike-slip fault |
| ____ **15.** Rocky Mountains | **c.** normal fault |

*Match the term with its definition.*

**Term**

____ **16.** anticline

____ **17.** syncline

____ **18.** folded mountains

**Definition**

**a.** Fold in rock that bends upward

**b.** Parallel ridges and valleys

**c.** Fold in rock that bends downward

## Changing Earth's Surface

**19.** Circle the letter of the sentence that describes how a fault-block mountain is created.

   **a.** It is created by two normal faults.

   **b.** It is created by two reverse faults.

   **c.** It is created by a strike-slip fault.

   **d.** It is created by shearing.

**20.** Circle the letter of each mountain range that was caused by folding.

   **a.** Alps

   **b.** Himalayas

   **c.** Appalachian

   **d.** Great Basin

**21.** What is a plateau? _____

_____

# Earthquakes and Seismic Waves

*This section explains how energy from an earthquake travels through Earth, how it can be detected, and how the size of an earthquake can be measured.*

## Use Target Reading Skills

As you read about seismic waves, complete the graphic organizer by filling in the details.

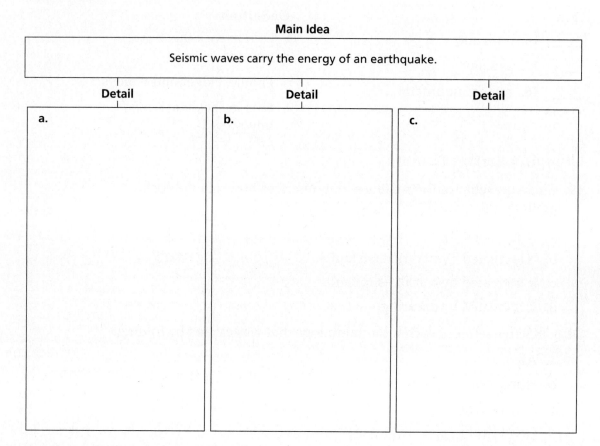

**Main Idea**

Seismic waves carry the energy of an earthquake.

| Detail | Detail | Detail |
|---|---|---|
| a. | b. | c. |

## Introduction

1. The point at which a rock under stress breaks and triggers an earthquake is called the _____.

2. The point on the surface directly above the focus is the

   _____.

## Types of Seismic Waves

3. What are seismic waves? _____

   _____

   _____

**Earthquakes** ▪ *Guided Reading and Study*

4. Is the following sentence true or false? Seismic waves carry the energy of an earthquake away from the focus in all directions.

   _____.

5. Circle the letter of each term that is a category of seismic wave.

   **a.** P wave

   **b.** S wave

   **c.** surface wave

   **d.** underground wave

6. Label each drawing as *S Waves* or *P Waves*.

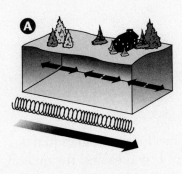 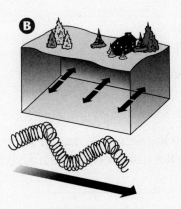

   _____          _____

7. Is the following sentence true or false? Surface waves move more quickly than P waves and S waves. _____

| Type of Wave | Effect |
|---|---|
| ____ 8. P wave | **a.** shakes buildings from side to side |
| ____ 9. S wave | **b.** shakes buildings violently |
| ____ 10. Surface wave | **c.** causes buildings to contract and expand |

11. A device that records the ground movements caused by seismic waves

    is a(n) _____.

**Earthquakes** ▪ *Guided Reading and Study*

# Earthquakes and Seismic Waves *(continued)*

## Measuring Earthquakes

12. List the three scales that are used for measuring earthquakes.

   a. _____

   b. _____

   c. _____

13. Circle the letter of the term that refers to the strength of earthquakes as measured by seismic waves and movement along faults.

   a. Richter value

   b. magnitude

   c. Mercalli force

   d. vibrations

## Locating the Epicenter

14. Is the following sentence true or false? The closer an earthquake, the greater the time between the arrival of P waves and the arrival

   of S waves. _____

15. Geologists use circles to find the epicenter of an earthquake.

   a. What does the center of each circle represent? _____

   _____

   b. What does the radius of each circle represent? _____

   _____

**Earthquakes** · *Guided Reading and Study*

# Monitoring Earthquakes

*This section explains how geologists monitor faults to try to predict earthquakes.*

## Use Target Reading Skills

As you read about seismographs, make a flowchart that shows how a seismograph produces a seismogram.

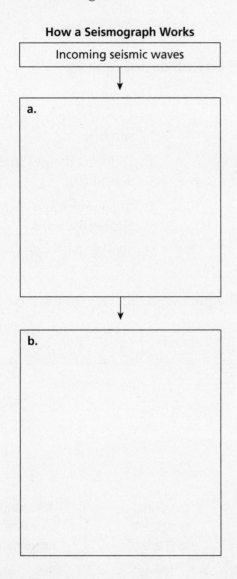

**How a Seismograph Works**

| Incoming seismic waves |

a.

b.

## The Modern Seismograph

1. How would you interpret a seismograph that shows only short jagged lines? _____

_____

**Earthquakes** · *Guided Reading and Study*

## Monitoring Earthquakes (*continued*)

2. List four instruments that geologists use to monitor movements along faults.

a. _____

b. _____

c. _____

d. _____

Match the type of monitoring device with its description.

**Monitoring Device**

____ 3. creep meter

____ 4. laser-ranging device

____ 5. tiltmeter

____ 6. GPS satellite

**Description**

a. Uses a network of Earth-orbiting satellites

b. Detects changes in distance to a reflector

c. Measures movement along a slip-strike fault

d. Works like a carpenter's level

7. Label each circle in the Venn diagram with the name of the monitoring device it represents.

a. _____     b. _____

Measures horizontal movement

Measures movement along a fault

Measures vertical movement

8. A device that bounces laser beams off a reflector to detect fault movements is a(n) _____.

9. A device that measures tiny movements of markers set up on the opposite sides of a fault is a(n) _____.

## Using Seismographic Data

10. How do seismic waves behave when they encounter a fault?

_____

11. How do the data from the movements of seismic waves help geologists determine the earthquake risk for an area? _____

_____

12. The force that opposes the motion of one surface as it moves across another surface is referred to as _____.

13. Is the following sentence true or false? Geologists can predict accurately where and when an earthquake will strike.

_____

**Earthquakes** • *Guided Reading and Study*

# Earthquake Safety

*This section explains how earthquakes cause damage. The section also describes how buildings can be constructed to withstand earthquakes and what people can do to help protect themselves from earthquakes.*

## Use Target Reading Skills

Complete the first column in the chart by previewing the red headings and asking a *what*, *how*, or *where* question for each. As you read the section, complete the second column with the answers.

**Earthquake Safety**

| Question | Answer |
|---|---|
| Where is quake risk highest? | Earthquake risk is highest . . . |
| | |
| | |
| | |

## Earthquake Risk

1.  What two factors do geologists take into account when they determine earthquake risk? _____

   _____

2.  Circle the letter of the location where the risk of earthquakes is highest in the United States.

   **a.** along the Gulf of Mexico

   **b.** along the Atlantic Coast

   **c.** along the Great Lakes

   **d.** along the Pacific Coast

**Earthquakes** · *Guided Reading and Study*

## How Earthquakes Cause Damage

3. What kinds of damage are caused by the severe shaking of an earthquake?

_____

_____

_____

_____

4. What determines where and how much the ground shakes?

_____

5. Is the following sentence true or false? A house built on solid rock will shake more during an earthquake than a house built on sandy soil.

_____

6. When an earthquake's violent shaking that turns loose, soft soil into

liquid mud is called _____. This process is likely to occur where the soil

is full of _____.

7. An earthquake that occurs after a larger earthquake in the same area is

referred to as a(n) _____.

8. Large ocean waves usually caused by strong earthquakes below the

ocean floor are called _____.

## Steps to Earthquake Safety

9. What is the main danger to people during an earthquake?

_____

10. Is the following sentence true or false? If no desk or table is available,

you should crouch against an outside wall. _____

11. Is the following sentence true or false? If you are outdoors during an earthquake, you should move under a tree or building.

_____

## Designing Safer Buildings

12. How can tall furniture be prevented from tipping over in an earthquake?

_____

# Earthquake Safety *(continued)*

13. How can bedrooms be made safer during an earthquake?

_____

_____

14. How can a brick or wood-frame building be modified to help it withstand an earthquake?

_____

_____

_____

15. What can be done when a new home is being built to help prevent damage caused by liquefaction?

_____

_____

16. How does a base-isolated building reduce the amount of energy that reaches the building during an earthquake?

_____

17. How can earthquakes cause fire and flooding?

_____

_____

**Earthquakes** · *Guided Reading and Study*

# ● Key Terms

*Read the clues below, and then find the key terms from the chapter that are hidden in the puzzle. The hidden terms may occur vertically, horizontally, or diagonally.*

## Clues

1. The shaking and trembling of Earth's crust

2. A fold in rock that bends downward

3. A stress force that squeezes rock

4. A large area of elevated flat land

5. A force that changes a rock's shape or volume

6. An earthquake that occurs after a larger earthquake in the same area

7. Large wave caused by earthquakes on the ocean floor

8. Stress that pushes rock in opposite directions

9. A fold in rock that bends upward

10. Occurs when an earthquake turns soil into liquid mud

11. The half of a fault that lies below

12. An instrument that records ground movements caused by seismic waves

```
s t i o n s c o d d l n p m
f a e a r t h q u a k e v l
w a f t e r s h o c k n d i
y t o n e e q u r c a f t q
d u p c o s h e a r i n g u
s w n o f s a z s e p t w e
e g o m i p h o r v a d t f
i n m p f g t p u l a c m a
s o d r s y n c l i n e p c
m w c e o m u a q a v b c t
o v e s j m w u c k t i b i
g l n s o t h u m b b e y o
r a t i o k v o o x l e a n
a w o o p l y i m s s a h u
p u f n t t s u n a m i s s
h a l e t a n t i c l i n e
```

# Connecting Concepts

Develop a concept map that uses the key concepts and key terms from this chapter. Keep in mind the main idea of this chapter: Forces inside Earth cause rocks to move and to release energy as seismic waves during an earthquake. The concept map shown is one way to organize how the information in this chapter is related. You may use an extra sheet of paper.

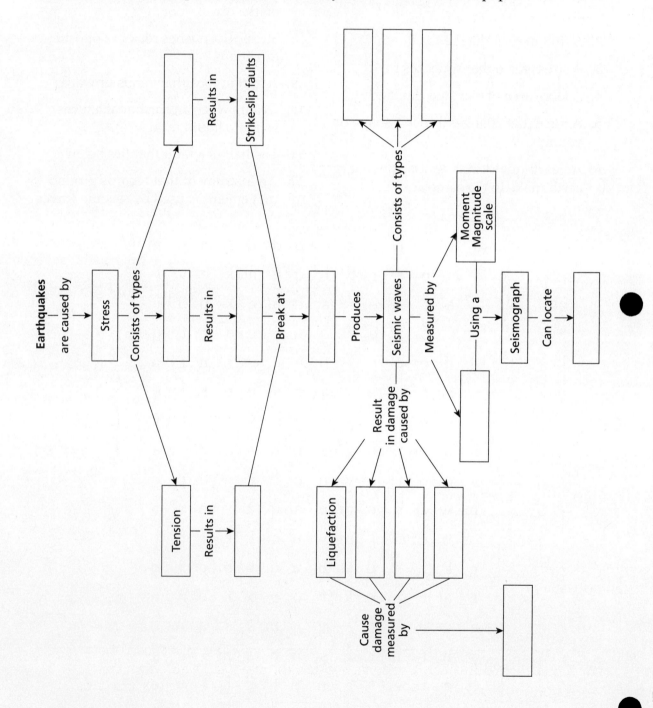

**Volcanoes** · *Guided Reading and Study*

# Volcanoes and Plate Tectonics

*This section explains what volcanoes are and identifies where most volcanoes occur.*

## Use Target Reading Skills

As you preview the headings in this section, complete the graphic organizer with questions in the left column. Then as you read, fill in the answers in the second column.

**Volcanoes and Plate Tectonics**

| Question | Answer |
|---|---|
| Where are volcanoes found? | Most volcanoes are found along plate boundaries. |
|  |  |

## Introduction

1. What is a volcano? _____

_____

_____

2. A molten mixture of rock-forming substances, gases, and water from the mantle is referred to as _____.

3. When magma reaches the surface, it is called _____.

Name _____ Date _____ Class_____

# Volcanoes and Plate Tectonics *(continued)*

## Volcanoes and Plate Boundaries

4. What is the Ring of Fire? _____

_____

_____

5. Where do most volcanoes form? _____

_____

_____

6. Describe how volcanoes form along the mid-ocean ridges. _____

_____

_____

7. Is the following sentence true or false? Volcanoes can form along

   diverging plate boundaries on land. _____

8. Is the following sentence true or false? Many volcanoes form near
   converging plate boundaries where oceanic crust returns to the mantle.

   _____

9. How does subduction at converging plate boundaries lead to the

   formation of volcanoes? _____

   _____

   _____

   _____

10. Volcanoes at boundaries where two oceanic plates collide create a string

    of islands called a(n) _____.

11. What are three major island arcs? _____

    _____

**Volcanoes** · *Guided Reading and Study*

12. Circle the letter of the types of plates that collided to form the Andes Mountains on the west coast of South America.

   a. two oceanic plates

   b. a continental plate and an oceanic plate

   c. a continental plate and an island plate

   d. two continental plates

## Hot Spot Volcanoes

13. What is a hot spot? _____

_____

_____

14. How did the Hawaiian Islands form? _____

_____

15. Is the following sentence true or false? Hot spots form only under

   oceanic crust. _____

_____

**Volcanoes** · *Guided Reading and Study*

# Properties of Magma

*This section explains physical and chemical properties, the property of viscosity, and the factors that determine the viscosity of magma.*

## Use Target Reading Skills

As you read about the viscosity of magma, fill in the detail boxes that explain the main idea in the graphic organizer below.

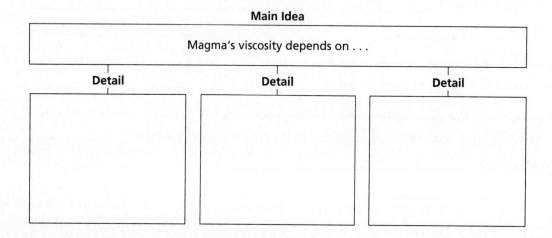

**Main Idea**

Magma's viscosity depends on . . .

Detail

Detail

Detail

## Physical and Chemical Properties

1. A substance that cannot be broken down into other substances is called

   a(n) _____.

2. Is the following sentence true or false? When frozen water melts, it is

   undergoing a physical change. _____

3. Circle the statements that indicate a chemical property.

   **a.** Water boils at 100°C under normal conditions.

   **b.** When paper is burned, it forms ashes.

   **c.** An iron chair will develop rust if oxygen combines with the iron.

   **d.** A basketball is larger than a baseball.

**Volcanoes** · *Guided Reading and Study*

## What Is Viscosity?

4. Fill in the blanks: The greater the viscosity, the _____ a liquid flows. The _____ the viscosity, the more easily a liquid flows.

5. Circle the liquids that have a relatively low viscosity.

   a. milk

   b. molasses

   c ketchup

   d. orange juice

   e. milkshake

## Viscosity of Magma

6. What factors determine the viscosity of magma? _____

   _____

7. Circle the letter of each sentence that is true about silica.

   a. It is formed from oxygen and nitrogen.

   b. It makes magma thicker.

   c. It is rarely found in the crust.

   d. It produces light-colored lava.

8. The rock _____ forms from light-colored lava.

9. Low-silica magma forms rocks like _____.

10. What happens to viscosity as temperature increases? _____

    _____

11. Hot, fast-moving lava is called _____.

12. Cool, slow-moving lava is called _____.

**Volcanoes** ▪ *Guided Reading and Study*

## Properties of Magma *(continued)*

**13.** Complete the compare/contrast table to organize the physical and chemical properties of the different types of magma.

| Viscosity of Magma | Temperature | Silica Content |
|---|---|---|
| High | b. | c. |
| a. | higher | d. |

**e.** State the relationship between temperature and silica content in magmas that have high viscosity and magmas that have low viscosity.

_____

_____

_____

_____

_____

**Volcanoes** · *Guided Reading and Study*

# Volcanic Eruptions

*This section explains how volcanoes erupt and describes types of volcanic eruptions as well as other types of volcanic activity. The section also describes how geologists monitor volcanoes and what hazards are associated with volcanoes.*

## Use Target Reading Skills

As you preview the section headings, write what you know about the topic in the box "What You Know." As you read the section, complete the "What You Learned" box.

| What You Know |
|---|
| I. Lava flows out of a volcano. |
| 2. |
| 3. |

| What You Learned |
|---|
| I. |
| 2. |
| 3. |

## Introduction

1. Is the following sentence true or false? Magma forms in the lithosphere.

_____

2. Is the following sentence true or false? Liquid magma rises until it reaches the surface, or until it becomes trapped beneath layers of rock.

_____

**Volcanoes** ▪ *Guided Reading and Study*

# Volcanic Eruptions *(continued)*

## Magma Reaches Earth's Surface

**3.** Circle the letter of each feature that all volcanoes share.

  **a.** pocket of magma beneath the surface

  **b.** crack to the surface

  **c.** side vents

  **d.** crater

**4.** Label the drawing with the following terms: magma chamber, pipe, vent, and crater.

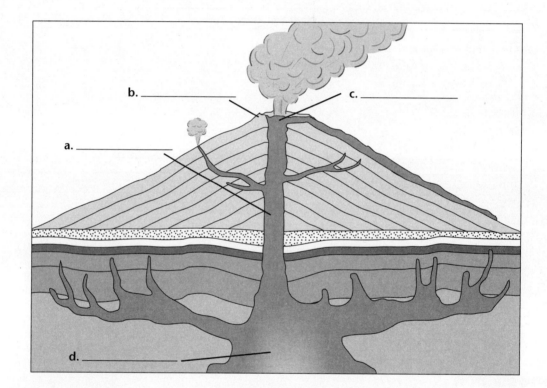

**5.** What is a lava flow? _____

_____

**6.** Where does a crater form? _____

_____

**7.** Is the following sentence true or false? The pipe of a volcano is a horizontal crack in the crust. _____

**Volcanoes** · *Guided Reading and Study*

8. Complete the flowchart showing in what sequence magma moves through a volcano.

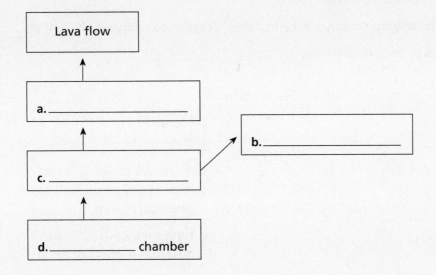

e. What does the graph show about where magma goes after it leaves the pipes?

_____

9. Circle the letter of the sentence that describes the best model of a volcano erupting.

   a. Carbon dioxide dissolved in soda pop rushes out when the pop is opened.

   b. A car goes faster when the accelerator is pushed.

   c. Water in a pot gets hotter when the pot is heated on a stove.

   d. Clay hardens when it is baked in an oven.

10. What happens during a volcanic eruption? _____

_____

_____

11. What factors determine the force of a volcanic eruption?

_____

_____

**Volcanoes** ▪ *Guided Reading and Study*

## Volcanic Eruptions *(continued)*

### Kinds of Volcanic Eruptions

12. Is the following sentence true or false? A volcano erupts quietly if its magma is thick and sticky. _____

Match the type of lava with its description.

| Type of Lava | Description |
|---|---|
| _____ 13. volcanic ash | **a.** Pebble-sized particles |
| _____ 14. cinders | **b.** Particles ranging from the size of a baseball to the size of a car |
| _____ 15. bombs | **c.** Fine rocky particles as small as a grain of sand |

16. What is a pyroclastic flow? _____

_____

17. Is the following sentence true or false? Volcanic eruptions cause damage only when they are close to the crater's rim. _____

18. What kinds of damage can volcanoes cause?

_____

_____

_____

### Stages of Volcanic Activity

19. Is the following sentence true or false? The activity of a volcano may last from less than a decade to more than 10 million years.

_____

20. Is the following sentence true or false? Most long-lived volcanoes erupt continuously. _____

**Volcanoes** ▪ *Guided Reading and Study*

**21.** Complete the compare/contrast table showing the different stages of a volcano.

| Volcanic Stages | |
|---|---|
| **Stage** | **Description** |
| a. | Unlikely to erupt ever again |
| b. | Erupting or showing signs that it soon will erupt |
| c. | No longer active but may become active again |

    **d.** Rank the volcanic stages from least likely to erupt to most likely to

       erupt: _____

**22.** Is the following sentence true or false? The length of time between eruptions of a dormant volcano is always less than a thousand years.

    _____

**23.** Why might people living near a dormant volcano be unaware of the

    danger? _____

    _____

**24.** Circle the letter of each sentence that is true about predicting volcanic eruptions.

    **a.** Geologists are more successful in predicting volcanic eruptions than earthquakes.

    **b.** There is never any warning when a volcano will erupt.

    **c.** Geologists can predict how powerful a volcanic eruption will be.

    **d.** Geologists cannot predict what type of eruption a volcano will produce.

**Volcanoes** • *Guided Reading and Study*

# Volcanic Landforms

*This section describes landforms and soils that are created by volcanoes, and types of geothermal activity.*

## Use Target Reading Skills

As you read about volcanic landforms, use the headings to complete the outline below.

| Volcanic Landforms |
| --- |

I. Landforms From Lava and Ash

   A. Shield Volcanoes

   B. _____

   C. _____

   D. Lava Plateaus

   E. _____

   F. _____

II. Landforms From Magma

   A. _____

   B. _____

   C. _____

   D. Dome Mountains

III. _____

   A. Hot Springs

   B. _____

   C. Geothermal Energy

Name _____ Date _____ Class _____

**Volcanoes** · *Guided Reading and Study*

## Landforms From Lava and Ash

1. List four landforms created from lava and ash.

    a. _____

    b. _____

    c. _____

    d. _____

2. Circle the letter of each sentence that is true about shield volcanoes.

    a. They form from many thin layers of lava.

    b. They result from quiet eruptions.

    c. They are very steep mountains.

    d. They are formed from ash, cinders, and bombs.

3. Is the following sentence true or false? The Hawaiian Islands are cinder cone volcanoes. _____

4. Name two examples of composite volcanoes. _____
    _____

5. Is the following sentence true or false? A composite volcano has both quiet and explosive eruption. _____

Name _____ Date _____ Class _____

# Volcanic Landforms *(continued)*

Match the landform with its description.

**Landform**

_____ **6.** shield volcano

_____ **7.** cinder cone

_____ **8.** composite volcano

_____ **9.** lava plateau

_____ **10.** caldera

**Description**

**a.** High, level area formed by repeated lava flows

**b.** Mountain formed by lava flows alternating with explosive eruptions

**c.** Cone-shaped mountain formed from ash, cinders, and bombs

**d.** Hole left by the collapse of a volcanic mountain

**e.** Gently sloping mountain formed by repeated lava flows

**11.** When volcanic ash breaks down, it releases _____ and _____, both of which are needed by plants.

## Landforms From Magma

**12.** List five features formed by magma.

   a. _____

   b. _____

   c. _____

   d. _____

   e. _____

**Volcanoes** · *Guided Reading and Study*

**13.** Complete the Venn diagram using the following phrases: forms from magma, forms across rock layers, forms between rock layers.

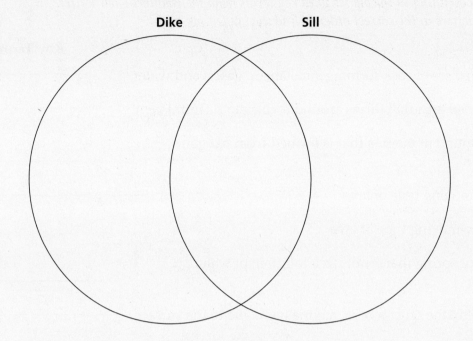

**Dike**                    **Sill**

**14.** A mass of rock formed when a large body of magma cools inside the crust is called a(n) _____.

**15.** What is an example of a batholith in the United States? _____
_____

**16.** Is the following sentence true or false? A dome mountain forms when rising magma is blocked by horizontal layers of rock. _____

## Geothermal Activity

**17.** Is the following sentence true or false? Some types of volcanic activity do not involve the eruption of lava.

**18.** When groundwater heated by a nearby body of magma rises to the surface and collects in a natural pool, it is called a(n) _____ .

**19.** A fountain of water and steam that erupts from the ground is referred to as a(n) _____ .

**20.** How can geothermal energy be converted to electricity? _____
_____
_____

**Volcanoes** · *Guided Reading and Study*

# Key Terms

*Solve the clues by filling in the blanks with key terms from the chapter. Then write the numbered letters in the correct order to find the hidden message.*

**Clues**                                                                                **Key Terms**

1. Molten mixture of rock-forming substances, gases, and water     $\underset{1}{—}\ —\ —\ \underset{2}{—}$

2. Bowl-shaped area that forms around a volcano's central vent     $—\ \underset{3}{—}\ —\ —\ —$

3. Material found in magma that is formed from oxygen and silicon     $\underset{4}{—}\ —\ —\ —\ —$

4. Hot, fast-moving type of lava     $—\ —\ \underset{5}{—}\ —\ —\ —\ —$

5. Cool, slow-moving type of lava     $—\ \underset{6}{—}$

6. Type of hot spring that erupts as a fountain of water and steam     $—\ —\ —\ \underset{7}{—}\ —\ —$

7. Weak spot in the crust where magma has come to the surface     $\underset{8}{—}\ —\ —\ —\ —\ \underset{9}{—}$

8. Magma that reaches the surface     $\underset{10}{—}\ —\ —$

9. Erupting or showing signs of erupting in the near future     $—\ \underset{11}{—}\ —\ —\ —$

10. Large hole at the top of a volcano     $—\ \underset{12}{—}\ —\ —\ —$

11. Unlikely to erupt again     $—\ —\ —\ —\ \underset{13}{—}\ —\ —$

12. Mass of rock formed when magma cooled inside the crust     $—\ —\ —\ \underset{14}{—}\ —\ —\ —$

13. Slab that forms when magma forces itself across rock layers     $—\ —\ —\ \underset{15}{—}$

14. Slab that forms when magma squeezes between layers of rock     $—\ —\ —\ \underset{16}{—}$

**Hidden Message**

$\underset{1}{—}\ \underset{2}{—}\ \underset{3}{—}\ \underset{4}{—}\quad \underset{5}{—}\ \underset{6}{—}\ \underset{7}{—}\quad \underset{8}{—}\ \underset{9}{—}\ \underset{10}{—}\ \underset{11}{—}\ \underset{12}{—}\ \underset{13}{—}\ \underset{14}{—}\ \underset{15}{—}\ \underset{16}{—}\ .$

# Connecting Concepts

Develop a concept map that uses the key concepts and key terms from this chapter. Keep in mind the big idea of this chapter: Forces inside Earth cause magma to heat, move, and push through the crust to erupt as volcanoes that pose hazards and form land features. The concept map shown is one way to organize how the information in this chapter is related. You may use an extra sheet of paper.

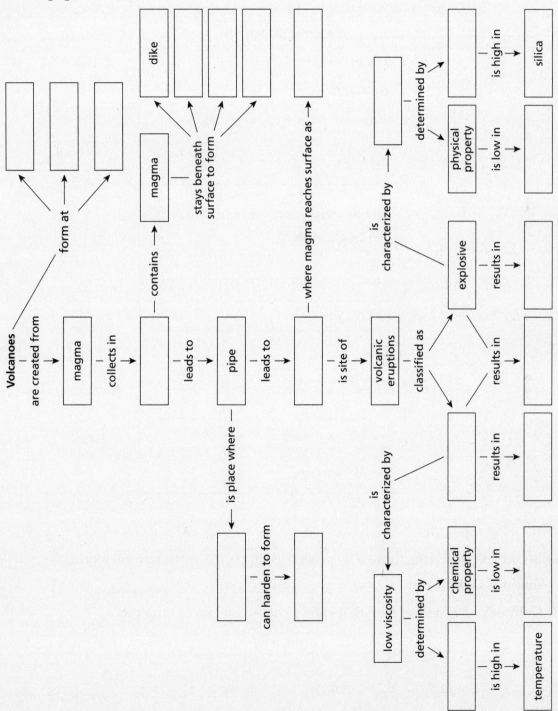

Name _____ Date _____ Class _____

**Minerals** · *Guided Reading and Study*

# Properties of Minerals

*This section explains what minerals are and how they can be identified.*

## Use Target Reading Skills

*As you read about properties of minerals, use the headings to complete the outline below.*

| Properties of Minerals |
|---|
| I. What Is a Mineral? |
| A. Naturally Occurring |
| B. Inorganic |
| C. _____ |
| D. _____ |
| E. _____ |
| II. Identifying Materials |
| A. Color |
| B. _____ |
| C. _____ |
| D. Density |
| E. _____ |
| F. _____ |
| G. _____ |
| H. Special Properties |

## What Is a Mineral?

1. Because minerals are formed by processes that occur in the natural world, they are said to be _____.

2. Complete the concept map that shows characteristics of minerals.

**Minerals** ▪ *Guided Reading and Study*

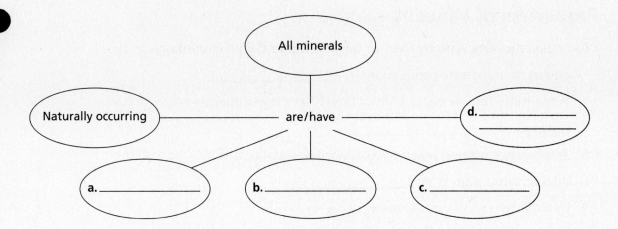

e. Use the concept map to write a definition of a mineral in your own words. You may use more than one sentence.

_____

_____

3. Because minerals do not come from living things, they are said to be

_____.

4. A substance that keeps its shape because its particles can't flow freely is

a(n) _____.

5. A solid with flat sides that meet at sharp edges and corners is called a(n)

_____.

**Minerals** ▪ *Guided Reading and Study*

# Properties of Minerals *(continued)*

6. Is the following sentence true or false? A mineral always contains certain elements in definite proportions. _____

7. Is the following sentence true or false? Very few minerals are compounds. _____

8. A substance formed when two or more elements combine and lose their distinct properties is a(n) _____.

9. In what two ways can elements occur in nature?

_____

10. What are some examples of minerals that occur as elements instead of compounds? _____

## Identifying Minerals

11. Is the following sentence true or false? Geologists have identified about 300 minerals. _____

12. Is the following sentence true or false? Each mineral has its own specific properties. _____

13. Why can't color alone be used to identify most minerals?

_____

_____

14. The color of a mineral's powder is its _____.

15. The term that describes how a mineral reflects light from its surface is _____.

16. Is the following sentence true or false? Minerals containing metals often have a shiny luster. _____

17. Circle the letter of each sentence that is true about the density of a mineral.

    a. A given mineral can have varying densities.

    b. The larger the sample of a mineral, the greater its density.

    c. Each mineral has a characteristic density.

    d. The density of a mineral is its mass divided by its volume.

**Minerals** · *Guided Reading and Study*

**18.** What is the Mohs hardness scale? _____

_____

**19.** The softest known mineral is _____. The hardest known

mineral is _____.

**20.** Is the following sentence true or false? A mineral can scratch any

mineral harder than itself. _____

**21.** Is the following sentence true or false? Each piece of a mineral has the

same crystal structure. _____

**22.** How do geologists classify crystal structures? _____

_____

_____

Match the term with its definition.

**Term**

____ **23.** cleavage

____ **24.** fracture

____ **25.** fluorescence

**Definition**

**a.** A mineral's ability to split easily along flat surfaces

**b.** A mineral's ability to glow under ultraviolet light

**c.** The way a mineral looks when it breaks

**Minerals** · *Guided Reading and Study*

# How Minerals Form

*This section describes how minerals form and where minerals are found.*

## Use Target Reading Skills

*As you preview the headings in this section, complete the graphic organizer with questions in the left column. As you read, fill in the answers in the second column.*

**Formation of Minerals**

| Question | Answer |
|---|---|
| How do minerals form from magma? | |
| | |

## Introduction

1. The process by which atoms are arranged to form a material with a crystal structure is referred to as _____.

2. In what two ways do minerals form?

   _____

   _____

   _____

## Minerals From Magma and Lava

3. What affects the size of crystals formed from magma? _____

   _____

   _____

   _____

**Minerals** ▪ *Guided Reading and Study*

**4.** Why does magma that cools deep below the surface have large crystals?

_____

_____

**5.** Is the following sentence true or false? Lava cools quickly and forms

minerals with small crystals. _____

## Minerals From Solutions

**6.** A mixture in which one substance dissolves in another is called a(n)

_____.

**7.** Is the following sentence true or false? Minerals can form when

solutions evaporate. _____

**8.** Circle the letter of each sentence that is true about halite deposits in the United States.

   **a.** Deposits are found in the Midwest and Southwest.

   **b.** Deposits are found along the Gulf Coast.

   **c.** Deposits formed over the past thousand years.

   **d.** Deposits formed when ancient seas evaporated.

**9.** How do minerals form from a hot water solution? _____

_____

_____

_____

_____

**10.** A narrow channel or slab of a mineral that is much different from the

surrounding rock is called a(n) _____.

**11.** How do veins form? _____

_____

_____

_____

**Minerals** • *Guided Reading and Study*

## How Minerals Form *(continued)*

12. Complete the Venn diagram by labeling the circles with the type of minerals they represent.

a. _____  b. _____

Form from melted materials    Form through crystallization    Form from dissolved materials

c. Use the Venn diagram to explain how formation of minerals is alike and different. _____

_____

_____

**Minerals** · *Guided Reading and Study*

# Using Mineral Resources

*This section describes the uses of minerals and how minerals are obtained.*

## Use Target Reading Skills

*As you come to each head in the section, stop and write what you know about that topic. As you read the passage, write what you learn.*

| What You Know |
|---|
| I. The gems used in jewelry are minerals.<br><br>2. |

| What You Learned |
|---|
| I.<br><br>2. |

## The Uses of Minerals

1. Any hard, colorful mineral that has a brilliant or glassy luster is called

    a(n) _____.

2. A gemstone that has been cut and polished is called a(n)

    _____.

**Minerals** • *Guided Reading and Study*

# Using Mineral Resources  *(continued)*

3. Circle the letter of each choice that is a way gems are used.

   a. jewelry

   b. fuel

   c. mechanical parts

   d. grinding and polishing

4. List four examples of metals.

   a. _____

   b. _____

   c. _____

   d. _____

5. Why are metals useful? _____

   _____

   _____

   _____

6. What are some uses of metals? _____

   _____

   _____

*Match each mineral with the product in which it is found.*

**Mineral**

____ 7. talc

____ 8. calcite

____ 9. quartz

____ 10. gypsum

**Product**

a. cement

b. microscopes

c. watches

d. powder

## Producing Metals From Minerals

11. A rock that contains a metal or economically useful mineral is called

    a(n) _____.

12. Is the following sentence true or false? Most metals occur in a pure form.

    _____

13. Much of the world's copper is contained in the mineral ore

    _____.

Name _____ Date _____ Class _____

**Minerals** · *Guided Reading and Study*

14. Anyone who searches for an ore deposit is called a(n) _____.

15. What features do geologists look for when they prospect for ores?

_____

_____

_____

16. Is the following sentence true or false? The map of an ore deposit helps miners decide how to mine the ore. _____

17. Complete the compare/contrast table to show the similarities and differences among the different types of ore deposits and mines.

| How Ores Are Mined | |
|---|---|
| **Kind of Ore Deposit** | **Type of Mine Used** |
| Starts near the surface and extends deep underground | a. |
| Occurs in veins | b. |
| Is exposed on the surface | c. |

d. Use the table to explain how the ore deposits removed by shaft mining and by strip mining are similar to the ore deposits removed in open pit mining. _____

_____

_____

_____

_____

18. Describe strip mining. _____

_____

_____

19. Describe open pit mining. _____

_____

_____

20. Describe a shaft mine. _____

_____

_____

**Minerals** · *Guided Reading and Study*

# Using Mineral Resources *(continued)*

**21.** The process in which an ore is melted to separate the useful metal from other elements is _____.

**22.** Is the following sentence true or false? People first developed smelting in the 1800s. _____

**23.** A solid mixture of two or more metals is called a(n)

_____.

**24.** Fill in the flowchart with the following steps in the correct sequence: produce carbon dioxide and molten iron, pour off molten iron, mix with limestone and coal, place in blast furnace.

**Smelting Iron Ore**

a. _____

↓

b. _____

↓

c. _____

↓

d. _____

Name _____ Date _____ Class _____

**Minerals** · *Guided Reading and Study*

# Key Terms

*Use the clues to help you unscramble the key terms from Chapter 4. Then put the numbered letters in order to find the answer to the riddle.*

**Clues**                                                     **Key Terms**

1. It's how it looks when it breaks.     tarfceur     _ _ _ _ _ _ _ (1)

2. It contains two or more metals.     ylaol     _ _ _ _ _ (2)

3. It could be shiny or pearly.     rutels     _ _ _ _ _ (3)

4. It was never alive.     rincanoig     _ _ _ _ _ _ _ _ _ (4)

5. It's the color of the powder.     rsaekt     _ _ _ _ _ _ (5)

6. It includes melting.     temsilgn     _ _ _ _ _ _ _ _ (6)

7. It has a repeating pattern.     ratlycs     _ _ _ _ _ _ _ (7)

8. It contains two or more elements.     pucnoodm     _ _ _ _ _ _ _ _ (8)

9. It's valued because it's beautiful and rare.     nsgoteem     _ _ _ _ _ _ _ _ (9)

10. It's a mixture.     situnloo     _ _ _ _ _ _ _ _ (10)

11. It's how it splits.     elagveac     _ _ _ _ _ _ _ _ (11)

12. It's composed of a single kind of atom.     teemlen     _ _ _ _ _ _ _ (12)

**Riddle:** Why do some minerals glow?

**Answer:** _ _ _ _ _ _ _ _ _ _ _ _
     1  2  3  4  5  6  7  8  9  10  11  12

# Connecting Concepts

Develop a concept map that uses the key concepts and key terms from this chapter. Keep in mind the big idea of this chapter: Minerals, formed by magma or by elements or compounds in hot solutions, share five characteristics that make them valuable resources. The concept map shown is one way to organize how the information in this chapter is related. You may use an extra sheet of paper.

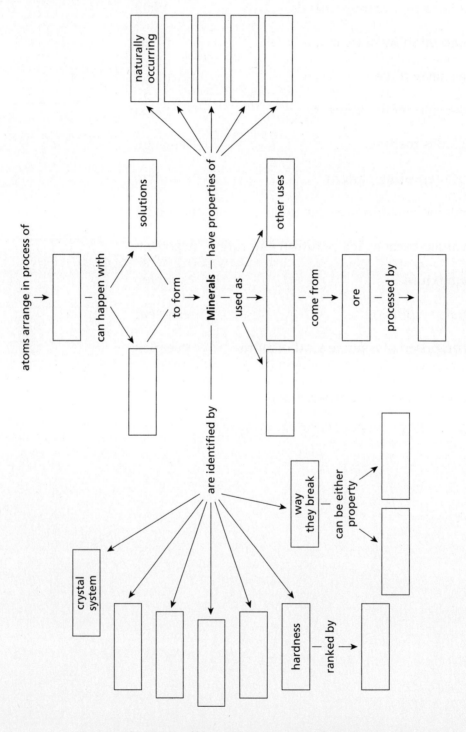

**Rocks** · *Guided Reading and Study*

# Classifying Rocks

*This section explains how geologists classify rocks.*

## Use Target Reading Skills

*As you preview the headings in this section, complete the graphic organizer with questions in the left column. Then as you read, fill in the answers in the second column.*

| Question | Answer |
|---|---|
| What does a rock's color tell about the rock? | |
| | |

## Introduction

1. Earth's crust is made of _____.

2. Circle the letter of each characteristic that geologists use to classify rocks.

    **a.** texture

    **b.** mineral composition

    **c.** hardness

    **d.** color

## Mineral Composition and Color

3. What are rocks made of? _____

   _____

   _____

4. Circle the letter of each mineral that is found in granite.

    **a.** quartz

    **b.** feldspar

    **c.** mica

    **d.** hornblende

**Rocks** · *Guided Reading and Study*

## Classifying Rocks *(continued)*

### Texture

5. Is the following sentence true or false? Most rocks can be identified by color alone. _____

6. The look and feel of a rock's surface is its _____.

7. Particles of minerals and other rocks that make up a rock are called

   _____.

8. Is the following sentence true or false? A rock's grains give the rock its texture. _____

9. Circle the letter of each sentence that is true about the grain size in rock.

   a. An example of a coarse-grained rock is diorite.

   b. An example of a fine-grained rock is slate.

   c. Grains in fine-grained rock are easy to see.

   d. Grains in coarse-grained rock are microscopic.

10. Complete the concept map showing the characteristics of rock texture.

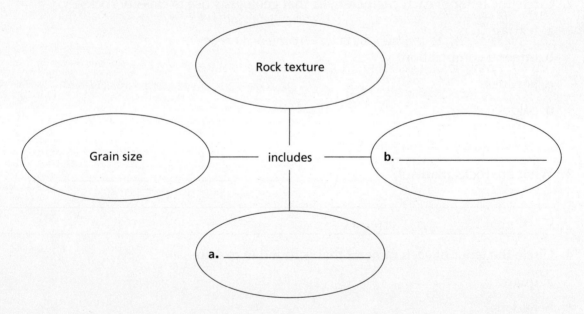

   c. Write a sentence that explains the relationship among the concepts shown.

   _____

   _____

**Rocks** · *Guided Reading and Study*

11. Circle the letter of the choice that determines the grain shape of a rock such as granite.

   **a.** Shape of the rock's crystals      **b.** Size of the rock's crystals

   **c.** Shape of fragments of other rock    **d.** Coarseness of the rock's grains

12. Circle the letter of the choice that determines the grain shape of a rock such as conglomerate.

   **a.** Shape of fragments of other rock    **b.** Size of the rock's grains

   **c.** Shape of the rock's crystals      **d.** Fineness of the rock's grains

13. Circle the letter of the description of the grain pattern of gneiss.

   **a.** It looks like different colors in bands.

   **b.** It looks like a stack of pancakes.

   **c.** It looks like waves.

   **d.** It looks like rows of squares and rectangles.

14. Circle the letter of the sentence that is true about rocks with no visible grain.

   **a.** Some rocks have no visible grain even under a microscope.

   **b.** Some rocks without crystal grains cooled very quickly.

   **c.** Rocks without crystal grains look rough and coarse.

   **d.** An example of a rock with a glassy texture is slate.

## How Rocks Form

15. How do geologists classify a rock? _____

   _____

   _____

16. List the three major groups of rock.

   **a.** _____

   **b.** _____

   **c.** _____

**Rocks** · *Guided Reading and Study*

## Classifying Rocks *(continued)*

17. Complete the compare/contrast table to show the similarities and differences among the types of rocks and how they form.

| How Rocks Form | |
| --- | --- |
| **Type of Rock** | **How It Forms** |
| a. | Molten rock cools. |
| b. | Particles are pressed and cemented. |
| c. | Existing rock is changed. |

    **d.** What do the three major types of rocks have in common? _____

_____

    **e.** How are they different? _____

_____

18. The type of rock that forms from magma or lava is _____ rock.

19. The type of rock that forms in layers is _____ rock.

20. Is the following sentence true or false? Most metamorphic rocks form close to the surface. _____

**Rocks** · *Guided Reading and Study*

# ● Igneous Rocks

*This section describes the characteristics and uses of igneous rocks.*

## Use Target Reading Skills

*As you read about igneous rocks, fill in the detail boxes that explain the main idea in the graphic organizer below.*

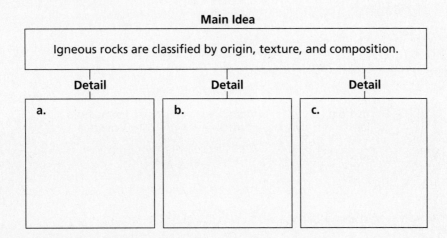

**Main Idea**

Igneous rocks are classified by origin, texture, and composition.

**Detail**  **Detail**  **Detail**

a.  b.  c.

## Classifying Igneous Rock

● 1. Circle the letter of the definition of igneous rock.

   **a.** Rock that forms from minerals

   **b.** Rock that contains iron

   **c.** Rock that forms from magma or lava

   **d.** Rock that contains crystals

**Rocks** · *Guided Reading and Study*

## Igneous Rocks *(continued)*

2. Complete the Venn diagram by labeling each circle with the type of rock it represents.

a. _____     b. _____

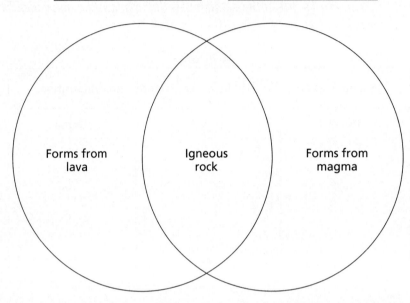

Forms from lava    Igneous rock    Forms from magma

c. Use the Venn diagram to explain how the types of rocks shown are

alike and different. _____

_____

3. Is the following sentence true or false? Extrusive rock forms beneath

Earth's surface. _____

4. Circle the letter of each sentence that is true about basalt.

   **a.** It forms much of the crust.

   **b.** It is the most common intrusive rock.

   **c.** It forms from lava.

   **d.** It forms beneath Earth's surface.

5. Circle the letter of each sentence that is true about granite.

   **a.** It is the most abundant intrusive rock in continental crust.

   **b.** It forms the core of many mountain ranges.

   **c.** It forms from magma.

   **d.** It forms on top of the crust.

6. The texture of an igneous rock depends on the size and shape of its

_____.

**Rocks** • *Guided Reading and Study*

7. Is the following sentence true or false? Igneous rocks with similar mineral compositions always have the same textures.

_____

Match the type of texture of igneous rocks with how rocks of that texture form.

| Type of Texture | How Rocks of That Texture Form |
|---|---|
| ____ 8. fine-grained | a. Magma cools in two stages. |
| ____ 9. coarse-grained | b. Lava cools rapidly. |
| ____ 10. porphyry rock | c. Magma cools slowly. |

11. Is the following sentence true or false? Intrusive rocks have smaller crystals than extrusive rocks. _____

12. A rock with large crystals surrounded by small crystals is called

_____.

13. What type of texture do extrusive rocks such as basalt have?

_____

_____

14. What is obsidian? _____

_____

15. Describe the texture of obsidian. _____

_____

16. Circle the letter of each sentence that is true about the silica composition of igneous rocks.

   a. Igneous rocks low in silica are usually dark-colored.

   b. An example of an igneous rock low in silica is granite.

   c. Igneous rocks high in silica are usually light-colored.

   d. An example of an igneous rock high in silica is basalt.

17. Describe the different minerals that determine the color of granite.

_____

_____

18. How do geologists determine the mineral composition of granite?

_____

_____

**Rocks** · *Guided Reading and Study*

## Igneous Rocks (continued)

### Uses of Igneous Rock

**19.** Why have people throughout history used igneous rocks for tools and building materials? _____

_____

**20.** Describe three ways granite has been used throughout history.

a. _____

b. _____

c. _____

**21.** Complete the table that shows the ways igneous rocks are used.

| How Some Igneous Rocks Are Used | |
| --- | --- |
| **Type of Igneous Rock** | **Way It Is Used** |
| Basalt | Gravel for construction |
| a. | Cleaning and polishing |
| b. | Soil mixes |

c. Use the information in the table to draw a conclusion about the uses of igneous rocks. You may use more than one sentence.

_____

_____

_____

_____

**Rocks** · *Guided Reading and Study*

# ● Sedimentary Rocks

*This section describes how sedimentary rocks form and how they are classified and used.*

## Use Target Reading Skills

*As you read about sedimentary rocks, use the headings to complete the outline below.*

| Sedimentary Rocks |
|---|
| I. From Sediment to Rocks |
|    A. Erosion |
|    B. _____ |
|    C. _____ |
|    D. Cementation |
| II. Types of Sedimentary Rock |
|    A. _____ |
|    B. Organic Rocks |
|    C. _____ |
|    D. _____ |
| III. _____ |

## From Sediment to Rock

1. What remains of living things may sediment include? _____

   _____

   _____

2. Small, solid pieces of material that come from rocks or living things are called _____.

3. Is the following sentence true or false? Sedimentary rocks form from particles deposited by water and wind. _____

**Rocks** ▪ *Guided Reading and Study*

## Sedimentary Rocks *(continued)*

**4.** List three forces that can carry sediment.

    **a.** _____

    **b.** _____

    **c.** _____

Match the process with its description.

| Process | Description |
|---|---|
| ____ **5.** erosion | **a.** Dissolved minerals glue sediments together. |
| ____ **6.** deposition | **b.** Sediments are pressed together in layers. |
| ____ **7.** compaction | **c.** Water or wind loosen and carry away fragments of rock. |
| ____ **8.** cementation | **d.** Sediments settle out of water or wind. |

**9.** What happens to rock fragments and other materials carried by water?

_____

_____

**10.** The process in which thick layers of sediment press down on the layers

beneath them is called _____.

**11.** Complete the flowchart to show how sediment is turned into sedimentary rock and what happens to it at each step.

**Sedimentary Rock Formation**

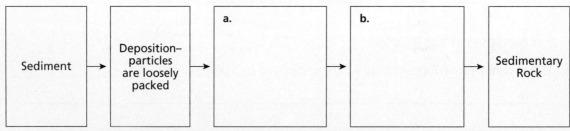

    **c.** Describe what happens to sediment as it is changed to sedimentary

    rock. _____

_____

**12.** Is the following sentence true or false? It takes millions of years for

sedimentary rock to form. _____

**Rocks** • *Guided Reading and Study*

## Types of Sedimentary Rock

13. How do geologists classify sedimentary rock? _____

_____

14. List the three major groups of sedimentary rock.

   a. _____

   b. _____

   c. _____

15. Is the following sentence true or false? The same process forms all types

   of sedimentary rock. _____

16. Is the following sentence true or false? Clastic rocks form when rock

   fragments are squeezed together. _____

17. How are clastic rocks classified? _____

_____

_____

18. Complete the table to show the different materials from which clastic
   rock forms.

| How Clastic Rock Forms | |
| --- | --- |
| **Type of Clastic Rock** | **Material From Which It Forms** |
| a. | Tiny particles of clay |
| b. | Small particles of sand |
| c. | Different-sized rock fragments |

   d. How are the types of clastic rocks shown in the table similar and

      different? _____

   _____

19. The type of rocks that form where the remains of plants and animals are

   deposited in thick layers is called _____ rock.

**Rocks** • *Guided Reading and Study*

## Sedimentary Rocks *(continued)*

**20.** List two important organic rocks.

   **a.** _____

   **b.** _____

**21.** Organic rock that forms from the remains of swamp plants buried in

water is _____ .

**22.** How does organic limestone form? _____

_____

_____

_____

_____

_____

**23.** Circle the letter of each sentence that describes a way that chemical rocks
can form.

   **a.** Minerals that are dissolved in a solution crystallize.

   **b.** Sediments of plants and animals form oil and other chemicals in rock.

   **c.** Mineral deposits form when seas or lakes evaporate.

   **d.** Tiny particles of clay are cemented together with chemicals.

**24.** Is the following sentence true or false? Some limestone is considered to

be a chemical rock. _____

**25.** Rock salt crystallizes from the mineral _____.

**Rocks** • *Guided Reading and Study*

## Uses of Sedimentary Rocks

**26.** Why have sandstone and limestone been used as building materials for thousands of years? _____

_____

_____

**27.** Is the following sentence true or false? The White House in Washington, D.C., is built of limestone. _____

**28.** What are some ways that builders today use sandstone and limestone?

_____

_____

_____

**29.** Is the following sentence true or false? Limestone is used for making cement. _____

**Rocks** • *Guided Reading and Study*

# Rocks From Reefs

*This section explains how coral reefs form and how coral reefs can become limestone deposits.*

## Use Target Reading Skills

*As you preview the section headings, write what you know about the topic in the box "What You Know." As you read the section, complete the "What You Learned" box.*

| What You Know |
|---|
| I. Coral reefs grow in the oceans. |
| 2. |
| 3. |

| What You Learned |
|---|
| I. |
| 2. |
| 3. |

## Coral Reefs

1. Circle the letter of each sentence that is true about living coral.

   a. It is a tiny plant.

   b. It is related to jellyfish.

   c. It lives in deep oceans.

   d. It eats microscopic creatures.

2. Skeletons of living coral grow together to form a structure called a(n) _____.

**Rocks** • *Guided Reading and Study*

3. Is the following sentence true or false? Almost all growth in a coral reef occurs close to the water's surface. _____

4. Coral animals absorb the element _____ from ocean water.

5. The protective outer shells of coral animals are formed from

   _____.

6. Circle the letter of each sentence that is true about coral reefs.

   a. They form only in cool water.

   b. They form only in tropical oceans.

   c. They form their skeletons by absorbing calcium.

   d. They form only in deep water.

7. Where are coral reefs most abundant? _____

   _____

   _____

   _____

8. In the United States, where are the only living coral reefs found? _____

   _____

   _____

9. Circle the letter of each sentence that is true about the growth of coral reefs.

   a. Coral reefs may grow to be hundreds of kilometers long.

   b. Coral reefs may grow to be hundreds of kilometers thick.

   c. Coral reefs usually grow inward away from the open ocean.

   d. Coral reefs may grow for thousands of years.

**Rocks** · *Guided Reading and Study*

## Rocks From Reefs *(continued)*

**10.** How do limestone deposits provide evidence of how plate motions have changed Earth's surface? _____

_____

_____

_____

_____

**11.** Where in the United States are ancient coral reefs preserved in rock? _____

_____

_____

**Rocks** · *Guided Reading and Study*

# Metamorphic Rocks

*This section explains how metamorphic rocks form, how they are classified, and how they are used.*

## Use Target Reading Skills

*Look at Figure 17 and write two questions you have about the visuals in the graphic organizer below. As you read about metamorphic rocks, write the answers to your questions.*

| | |
|---|---|
| **Q.** Why do the crystals in gneiss line up in bands? | |
| **A.** | |
| **Q.** | |
| **A.** | |

## Introduction

1. List the two forces that can change rocks into metamorphic rocks.

    a. _____

    b. _____

**Rocks** • *Guided Reading and Study*

# Metamorphic Rocks *(continued)*

2. Is the following sentence true or false? Metamorphic rocks form deep beneath Earth's surface. _____

3. How do rocks change when they become metamorphic rocks?

   _____

   _____

4. What kinds of rocks can be changed into metamorphic rocks?

   _____

   _____

5. Is the following sentence true or false? The deeper a rock is buried in the crust, the less pressure there is on that rock. _____

## Types of Metamorphic Rocks

6. Is the following sentence true or false? Geologists classify metamorphic rocks by the arrangement of grains making up the rocks.

   _____

7. Metamorphic rocks with grains arranged in parallel layers or bands are said to be _____.

8. Circle the letter of each type of metamorphic rock that is foliated.

   **a.** slate

   **b.** schist

   **c.** gneiss

   **d.** marble

9. Metamorphic rocks with grains arranged randomly are said to be

   _____.

10. List two examples of nonfoliated metamorphic rocks.

    **a.** _____

    **b.** _____

**Rocks** ▪ *Guided Reading and Study*

**11.** Complete the flowchart to show the metamorphic rocks that are formed.

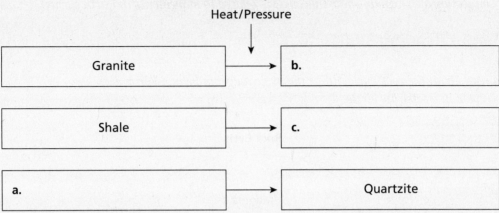

**How Some Metamorphic Rocks Form**

Heat/Pressure

| Granite | → | b. |

| Shale | → | c. |

| a. | → | Quartzite |

**d.** What does the flow chart show is happening to the rocks to the left?

_____

_____

## Uses of Metamorphic Rock

**12.** Why is marble useful for buildings and statues? _____

_____

_____

**13.** What are some of the ways that slate is used? _____

_____

_____

**Rocks** · *Guided Reading and Study*

# The Rock Cycle

*This section describes the cycle that builds, destroys, and changes rocks in Earth's crust. The section also explains how this cycle is related to movements in Earth's crust.*

## Use Target Reading Skills

*As you read about the rock cycle, fill in the cycle diagram below. Write each stage of the rock cycle in a separate circle.*

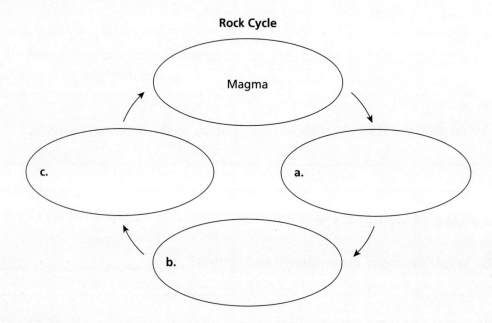

## Introduction

1. What forces move rocks through the rock cycle?

   _____

   _____

**Rocks** · *Guided Reading and Study*

2. The series of processes that slowly change rocks from one kind to another is referred to as the _____.

3. Is the following sentence true or false? All rocks follow the same pathway through the rock cycle. _____

4. How could granite be changed into sandstone? _____

   _____

   _____

   _____

## The Rock Cycle and Plate Tectonics

5. How do plate movements drive the rock cycle? _____

   _____

   _____

   _____

   _____

# Key Terms

*Test your knowledge of rocks by using key terms from the chapter to solve the crossword puzzle.*

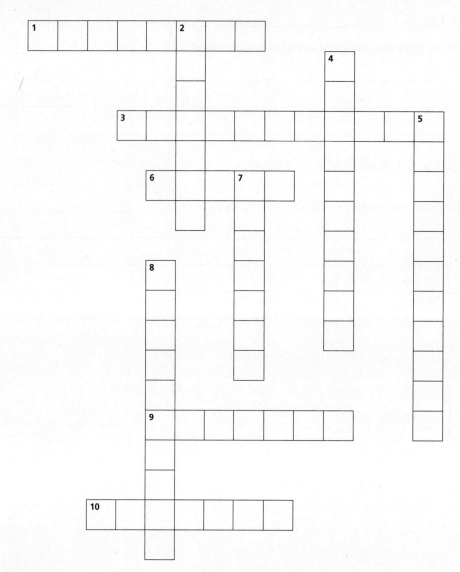

**Clues across**

1. Rocks with grains arranged in parallel layers
3. Rock formed by heat or pressure
6. Particle that gives rock texture
9. Sedimentary rock formed under pressure
10. Movement of fragments of rock

**Clues down**

2. Look and feel of a rock's surface
4. Process in which sediment is deposited in layers
5. Process of gluing sediments
7. Rock formed from molten rock
8. Process of pressing sediments

Name _____  Date _____  Class _____

**Rocks** ▪ *Guided Reading and Study*

# Connecting Concepts

Develop a concept map that uses the key concepts and key terms from this chapter. Keep in mind the big idea of this chapter: Rocks are classified into three main categories and undergo changes through a process called the rock cycle. The concept map shown is one way to organize how the information in this chapter is related. You may use an extra sheet of paper.

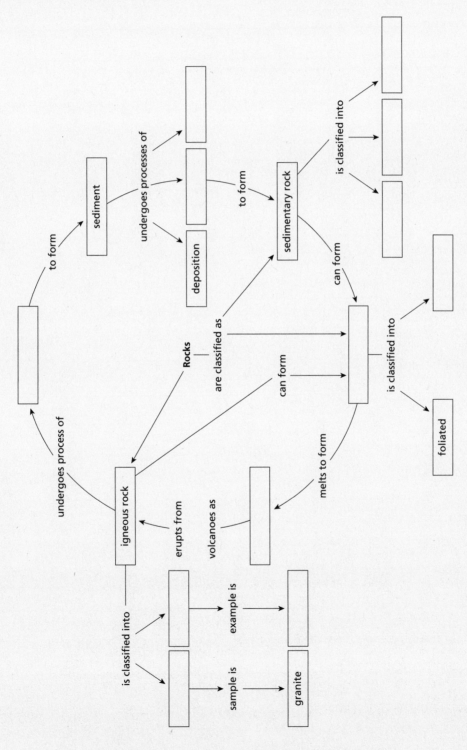